INSIDE MAJOR LEAGUE BASEBALL™

BASEBALL IN THE
NATIONAL LEAGUE CENTRAL
DIVISION

CHICAGO

CUBS

CINCINNATI

REDS

HOUSTON

ASTROS

MILWAUKEE

BREWERS

PITTSBURGH

PIRATES

ST. LOUIS

CARDINALS

rosen publishing's
rosen central®

New York

ED ECK

Published in 2009 by The Rosen Publishing Group, Inc.
29 East 21st Street, New York, NY 10010

First Edition

Library of Congress Cataloging-in-Publication Data

Eck, Ed.
Baseball in the National League Central Division / Ed Eck.—1st ed.
    p. cm.—(Inside major league baseball)
Includes bibliographical references and index.
ISBN-13: 978-1-4358-5045-3 (library binding)
ISBN-13: 978-1-4358-5419-2 (pbk)
ISBN-13: 978-1-4358-5425-3 (6 pack)
1. National League of Professional Baseball Clubs—History—Juvenile literature.
2. Baseball teams—United States—Juvenile literature. I. Title.
GV875.A3E245 2009
796.357—dc22

                                                                    2008026339

Manufactured in the United States of America

On the cover: On baseball cards, top to bottom: Alfonso Soriano of the Chicago Cubs; Adam Harang of the Cincinnati Reds; Roy Oswalt of the Houston Astros; Prince Fielder of the Milwaukee Brewers; Nate McLouth of the Pittsburgh Pirates; and Chris Carpenter of the St. Louis Cardinals. Background: Wrigley Field in Chicago. Foreground: Albert Pujols of the St. Louis Cardinals.

INTRODUCTION

In 2006, the St. Louis Cardinals and Detroit Tigers faced off in the World Series. The Tigers had caught fire in the play-offs, crushing the New York Yankees and sweeping the Oakland A's on their way to the American League title. The Cardinals were a different story. They won their weak division with only 83 regular season victories—the fewest wins of any team to make the play-offs in 2006. However, the team showed a knack for winning games when it counted. As a result, they found themselves in the World Series for the second time in three years.

The teams split the first two games of the series. Then, St. Louis surprisingly won the third and fourth games, leaving them only one win away from a World Series championship. Game 5 was played at Busch Stadium, the Cardinals' new ballpark, which had opened just that year. More than 46,000 fans packed the stadium, nearly all of them dressed in Cardinal red and rooting for their hometown team.

Cardinals starting pitcher Jeff Weaver held the Tigers to two runs in eight innings, and in the ninth inning, Cardinals rookie Adam Wainwright was brought in to close out the game. Tension mounted throughout Busch Stadium, as Wainwright pitched himself into a little jam. But finally, with runners on first and third and the go-ahead run at the plate, Wainwright dramatically struck out the Tigers' Brandon Inge. The Cardinals were World Series champs once again!

Since baseball realigned its teams in 1994, the Cardinals

Background: Busch Stadium on Opening Day, April 1, 2007. Above: Cardinals pitcher Adam Wainwright reacts after defeating the Detroit Tigers in game 5 of the 2006 World Series.

have played in the Central division of the National League (NL). The NL Central is unlike any of the other five divisions in Major League Baseball (MLB). It is a recent creation, but several of its teams have long, storied histories. The rivalry between the Cubs and Cardinals franchises, for example, dates back more than 120 years. Take the division's longstanding traditions, mix in plenty of zealous fans and a slew of excellent players, and you have a recipe for exciting baseball, year after year.

CHAPTER ONE
HISTORY OF THE NL CENTRAL

Teams in the National League Central division are among the oldest in baseball. In fact, the Cincinnati Reds team was the first professional baseball team ever. As the Cincinnati Red Stockings, they became a strictly professional team in 1869. Within a decade, the professional National League was formed.

In 1901, the rival American League began playing. Two years later, the champions of the

Above, left: Roberto Clemente, the 1966 National League Most Valuable Player. Clemente played his entire career with the Pittsburgh Pirates, from 1955 to 1972.

National League played the champions of the American League in the first World Series. This event began the modern era of baseball. Some teams joined the leagues and others failed, but the basic structure of the leagues remained the same for decades: two leagues with about eight teams in each.

Expansion Splits the National League

The U.S. population grew quickly in the 1940s and 1950s, and the popularity of baseball grew along with it. By the early 1960s, fans in cities around the country were clamoring for their own major league teams. As a result, in 1962, the National League expanded from eight to ten teams, and in 1969, it expanded again. Now with 12 teams, the National League was split into two six-team divisions, East and West. This new setup required an extra round of play-offs. So, starting in 1969, the best team in the East division played the best team from the West division in the new National League Championship Series (NLCS).

National League Central Champs
(since 1994 realignment)

1994: Cincinnati Reds*
1995: Cincinnati Reds
1996: St. Louis Cardinals
1997: Houston Astros
1998: Houston Astros
1999: Houston Astros
2000: St. Louis Cardinals
2001: Houston Astros
2002: St. Louis Cardinals
2003: Chicago Cubs
2004: St. Louis Cardinals
2005: St. Louis Cardinals
2006: St. Louis Cardinals
2007: Chicago Cubs
* Strike-shortened season; no play-offs.

In 1972, the Cincinnati Reds battled the Pittsburgh Pirates in the National League Championship Series. In the deciding game 5, Reds catcher Johnny Bench *(at bat)* hit a ninth-inning home run to tie the game at 3–3. The Reds went on to win the game 4–3 to advance to the World Series.

The winner of that series advanced to the World Series to take on the winners of the American League Championship Series (ALCS). With a couple of changes, this was the system used until 1994.

The Current System

In 1993, the National League added two more teams, bringing the total number of NL teams to 14. Then, in 1994, the Central division

NATIONAL LEAGUE CENTRAL CITIES

MILWAUKEE •
CHICAGO •
PITTSBURGH •
• CINCINNATI
ST. LOUIS •
HOUSTON •

Area of Detail Shown

CANADA

UNITED STATES

MEXICO

Five of the six teams in the National League Central division are bunched together near the Great Lakes region. Houston, for its part, is located a bit farther south, near the Gulf of Mexico.

was created, and the National League became a three-division league. The Cincinnati Reds and Houston Astros moved from the NL West to the NL Central, joining the Chicago Cubs, Pittsburgh Pirates, and St. Louis Cardinals, all from the NL East. This logical new arrangement grouped teams from the same area of the United States within the same division.

National League Central Team History
(since realignment in 1994)

	YEAR ENTERED NL CENTRAL	NL CENTRAL CHAMPIONSHIPS	NATIONAL LEAGUE PENNANTS	WORLD SERIES CHAMPIONSHIPS
Chicago Cubs	1994	2	0	0
Cincinnati Reds	1994	2*	0	0
Houston Astros	1994	4	1	0
Milwaukee Brewers	1998	0	0	0
Pittsburgh Pirates	1994	0	0	0
St. Louis Cardinals	1994	7	2	1

* Includes 1994; Cincinnati was leading the division when the season was cut short by the players' strike.

The new team alignment required another change in the play-off system. Now, the three divisional champs and one wild card team make it to the first round of play-offs, called the National League Division Series (NLDS). The winners of the two NLDS meet in the National League Championship Series to decide who plays in the World Series.

Change came to the National League once again in 1998. One more team was added, and the Milwaukee Brewers moved from the American League East to the National League Central, in order to provide balance for league scheduling.

Since the beginning of the three-division format, most teams in the NL Central division have enjoyed some success. The Reds, for example, advanced as far as the NLCS in 1995. The Astros put together some impressive teams in the 1990s, winning three straight NL Central titles (1997, 1998, and 1999) and making it to the World Series in 2004. The Cubs made it to the play-offs twice, in 1998 and 2003, but could not advance to the World Series.

Astros second baseman Craig Biggio prepares to turn a double play, as the Cubs' César Izturis slides hard into the bag. Until 1994, the Astros and Cubs played in different divisions.

As of 2007, the best NL Central team was the 2006 St. Louis squad, which beat the Detroit Tigers in the World Series.

In recent years, the NL Central has been dominated by the Astros, the Cubs, and especially the Cardinals. But one of the great things about baseball is that the beginning of each season brings with it a fresh start and new hope, for fans and players alike. Since realignment in 1994, neither the Pittsburgh Pirates nor the Milwaukee Brewers have managed to win the NL Central division title, and the Cincinnati Reds last won the division series in the mid-1990s. However, these three teams are loaded with young, talented baseball players, and it is probably just a matter of time before they are regularly contending for the division championship.

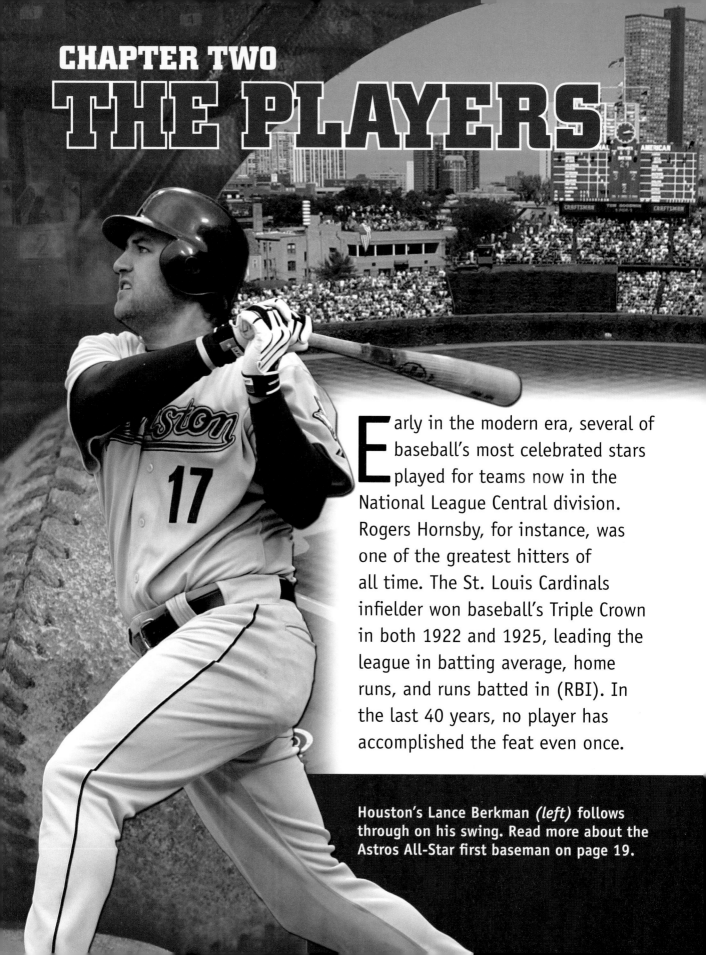

CHAPTER TWO

THE PLAYERS

Early in the modern era, several of baseball's most celebrated stars played for teams now in the National League Central division. Rogers Hornsby, for instance, was one of the greatest hitters of all time. The St. Louis Cardinals infielder won baseball's Triple Crown in both 1922 and 1925, leading the league in batting average, home runs, and runs batted in (RBI). In the last 40 years, no player has accomplished the feat even once.

Houston's Lance Berkman *(left)* follows through on his swing. Read more about the Astros All-Star first baseman on page 19.

In addition to Hornsby, Honus Wagner of the Pirates and Stan Musial of the Cardinals are among baseball's all-time greats. Later, in the 1950s and 1960s, teams now in the Central Division featured such Hall of Fame stars as Roberto Clemente (Pittsburgh), Lou Brock and Bob Gibson (St. Louis), Frank Robinson (Cincinnati), and Ernie Banks (Chicago). Top stars from the 1970s and 1980s include Willie Stargell (Pittsburgh); Johnny Bench, Joe Morgan, and Pete Rose (Cincinnati); Nolan Ryan (Houston); Paul Molitor and Robin Yount (Milwaukee); and Ryne Sandberg (Chicago). The greatest slugger of all time, Barry Bonds, played for Pittsburgh from 1986 to 1992. He won his first two National League MVP Awards while playing with the Pirates, prior to moving to the San Francisco Giants.

All of these special players separated themselves from the pack. The players profiled in this chapter are some of those who have risen above the rest since the creation of the NL Central division in 1994.

Jeff Bagwell and Craig Biggio (Astros)

For years, Jeff Bagwell and Craig Biggio were the cornerstones of the Houston Astros organization. A four-time All-Star, Bagwell played his entire career with the Astros. In 1991, he won the National League Rookie of the Year Award. It turned out that the big first baseman was just getting warmed up. In the strike-shortened season of 1994, "Bags" put together a fantastic year, earning a Gold Glove Award at first base and taking home the 1994 National League MVP Award. Between 1994 and 2004, Bagwell averaged an incredible 115 runs scored, 35 home runs, and 113 RBI. He retired after the 2005 season.

Like Jeff Bagwell, Craig Biggio played his entire big league career with the Houston Astros. Biggio made the All-Star team seven times and earned four Gold Glove Awards at second base. Year after year, when Bagwell was among the league leaders in RBI, it was often Biggio who was scoring the runs. Throughout his career, Biggio was consistently among the league leaders in runs scored, hits, and doubles. Biggio retired in 2007 with more than 3,000 career hits.

Ken Griffey Jr. (Reds)

From 2000 to 2008, the NL West was home to Ken Griffey Jr. "Junior," as he is known, is the son of Ken Griffey Sr., a former Cincinnati Reds star. The younger Griffey first played for Seattle in the American League, becoming one of the best all-around players in the game. After the 1999 season, Seattle traded Griffey to the Reds, who welcomed the Cincinnati native with open arms. In 2008, Junior hit his 600th career home run, a plateau reached by only five others in MLB history. *(See opposite page.)* Griffey joined the Chicago White Sox in July 2008.

Albert Pujols (Cardinals)

When talking about baseball's best all-around hitters, nearly everyone puts Cardinals All-Star first baseman Albert Pujols at the top of the list. He is regularly among the league leaders in batting average, runs scored, hits, total bases, home runs, RBI, and walks.

Originally from the Dominican Republic, Pujols burst on the MLB scene in a big way in 2001. He batted .329, hitting 37 home runs and knocking in 130 runs. With those numbers, he ran away with the 2001 National League Rookie of the Year Award. In 2005, Pujols won the National League MVP Award, and he has been a top contender for

While playing for the Cincinnati Reds, Ken Griffey Jr. connected for his historic 600th career home run, on June 9, 2008. Along with the great Ted Williams, Griffey is often named as the player with the "sweetest" swing ever.

MVP in several other years as well. St. Louis manager Tony La Russa, whose baseball career spans more than 45 years, says that Pujols is the best hitter he has ever seen.

Derrek Lee (Cubs)

When the Cubs are looking for a big hit, they usually look to their big

Derrek Lee of the Chicago Cubs makes a catch during a 2007 game at Wrigley Field. For a big man (he stands six feet five inches), Lee is especially agile in the field.

first baseman, Derrek Lee. Lee is a great all-around athlete with a good baseball pedigree: his father, Leon, and uncle Leron were both American players who starred in the Japanese professional league. Lee played six years with the Florida Marlins, winning a World Series title with them in 2003. He was then traded to the Cubs in 2004. In his second year with the Cubs, Lee led the National League with a .335 average and 50 doubles. The All-Star Lee is also a nimble fielder, winning three Gold Glove Awards between 2003 and 2007.

Upper Management

Fans pack the seats to see their favorite players on the field. But players don't get good on their own. They need a smart manager to help them reach their potential. One of the best managers in the game is the St. Louis Cardinals' Tony La Russa. Since taking over the Cardinals managing duties in 1996, La Russa has guided the team to the NL Central division title six times. The team made it all the way to the World Series in both 2004 and 2006 and won it all in 2006. La Russa also guided the American League's Oakland A's to the 1989 world championship. Only one other manager in history, Sparky Anderson, has won World Series titles in both leagues.

Many say that La Russa is the smartest manager in the game. In fact, his analytical style is cited as one of the biggest influences in changing the way the game is played nowadays. La Russa figured out that the big goal of winning baseball games often comes down to making many small decisions throughout a game. For example, if La Russa knows that a certain relief pitcher has great success against one batter in the opponent's lineup but not the next, he will bring in that pitcher to face just one batter. Two decades ago, this style of micromanaging was unheard of. However, La Russa has achieved great success with this approach, and, as a result, many others have followed his lead.

Lance Berkman (Astros)

Lance Berkman makes hitting look easy. However, those who have watched him develop know that he worked hard to perfect his smooth swing. In 2001, his second year with the Astros, the switch-hitting Berkman put it all together, batting .331 with 34 home runs and 126 RBI. His power hitting improved steadily after that year, and in 2006, he batted .315 with 45 home runs and 136 batted in. Berkman made the National League All-Star team five times in his first eight seasons.

Carlos Zambrano (Cubs)

Zambrano has played his entire career with the Cubs. Known for his wicked sinking fastball, the big right-handed ace tied for the NL lead with 16 wins in 2006. His 18 victories in 2007 were second only to Cy Young Award–winner Jake Peavy of the San Diego Padres. The fiery Venezuelan hurler is also a very good hitter, batting .300 in 2005. The following year, he became only the second Cubs pitcher ever to hit six

The Cubs' Carlos Zambrano delivers a pitch in a 2007 game at Wrigley Field. The reliable Zambrano started 34 games in 2007, tied for second most in the

home runs in one season. In 2008, he even recorded a four-hit game—a nice accomplishment for any player, never mind a pitcher.

Adam Dunn (Reds)

For eight years, slugger Adam Dunn was a fan favorite in Cincinnati. It may have had something to do with his easy smile and regular-guy attitude. And it probably didn't hurt that he launches eye-popping home runs with regularity. The big outfielder—he's six feet six and 275 pounds—was an excellent football player in high school and college. But as a professional athlete, he chose to play baseball instead. Dunn hit at least 40 big flies each season between 2004 and 2007. With his big swing, Dunn hits a lot of homers, but he also strikes out a lot. In fact, in 2004 he struck out 195 times, which set a single-season record at the time. In 2008, Dunn joined the Arizona Diamondbacks.

Roy Oswalt (Astros)

In 2001, first-year pitcher Roy Oswalt posted a very impressive 14–3 record, with a 2.73 earned run average (ERA). Since then, Oswalt has become one of the game's most reliable starters. Between 2001 and 2007, he earned more victories (112) than any other pitcher in the majors. In 2004, the Astros' All-Star ace was the only National League pitcher to reach 20 wins, a milestone he reached again in 2005.

Rising Stars

In addition to the bona fide veteran stars mentioned above, National League Central teams boast some of the best new players in the major leagues. Several of these young stars are discussed below. If these guys continue to play as they have in their first few years, then the division will be worth watching well into the future.

Prince Fielder (Brewers)

Milwaukee's Prince Fielder is the son of former Detroit Tigers home run king, Cecil Fielder. The younger Fielder caught the attention of many when, as legend has it, he hit a home run into the upper deck at old Tiger Stadium—at age 12! Now fully grown, the burly Brewers first baseman is one of the most dangerous hitters in the National League.

National League Central Award Winners
(since realignment in 1994)

National League MVP Award
1994 Jeff Bagwell (Astros)
1995 Barry Larkin (Reds)
1998 Sammy Sosa (Cubs)
2005 Albert Pujols (Cardinals)

National League Rookie of the Year Award
1998 Kerry Wood (Cubs)
1999 Scott Williamson (Reds)
2001 Albert Pujols (Cardinals)
2004 Jason Bay (Pirates)
2007 Ryan Braun (Brewers)

National League Cy Young Award
2004 Roger Clemens (Astros)
2005 Chris Carpenter (Cardinals)

Rolaids Relief Man of the Year Award
1995 Tom Henke (Cardinals)
1996 Jeff Brantley (Reds)
1997 Jeff Shaw (Reds)
1999 Billy Wagner (Astros)

World Series MVP Award
2006 David Eckstein (Cardinals)

In 2007, in just his second year in the big leagues, Fielder led the National League with 50 homers and made the All-Star team. After the 2007 season, Fielder changed to a vegetarian diet. In early 2008, Fielder told reporter Adam McCalvy of MLB.com, "Since I started [the new diet], I feel amazing." That's bad news for opposing pitchers.

Jason Bay (Pirates)

Not too many baseball insiders expected great things from Jason Bay when he was drafted in the 22nd round of the 2000 amateur draft. However, the scrappy outfielder quickly put any doubts to rest by winning the 2004 Rookie of the Year Award. In 2005, Bay was the only player in the major leagues to hit at least .300 with at least 40 doubles, 30 homers, 100 runs scored, 100 RBI, and 20 stolen bases. Unfortunately for Pittsburgh fans, Bay was traded to the Boston Red Sox in July 2008.

Brandon Phillips (Reds)

Phillips debuted with the Cleveland Indians but was traded to the Cincinnati Reds in 2006. In his second season in Cincinnati, the Reds infielder had his breakout season. He scored more than 100 runs and joined the exclusive 30–30 club, knocking out 30 home runs and swiping 32 bases.

Ryan Braun (Brewers)

Braun, the 2007 NL Rookie of the Year, led all first-year players in batting average (.324), extra base hits (66), and home runs (34). These numbers were especially impressive in light of the fact that he played in only 113 games. In 2008, Braun made his first NL All-Star team. His vote total (3,835,840) was second only to Philadelphia

Milwaukee Brewers left fielder Ryan Braun leaps to make a catch in a game against the Arizona Diamondbacks in 2008.

Phillies second baseman Chase Utley.

Aaron Harang (Reds)

Aaron Harang debuted with Oakland in the American League but was traded to Cincinnati in 2003. Within a couple years, the big right-hander was a dominant pitcher. In both 2006 and 2007, he earned 16 victories and was in the top five in the league in wins, innings pitched, strikeouts, and games started. In one of his more memorable outings in 2006, Harang held the St. Louis Cardinals scoreless into the eighth inning in a 1–0 Reds victory. One reason the game stood out was because Harang beat Cy Young Award–winner Chris Carpenter. A second reason? The winning run scored on a line-drive single by none other than Harang himself.

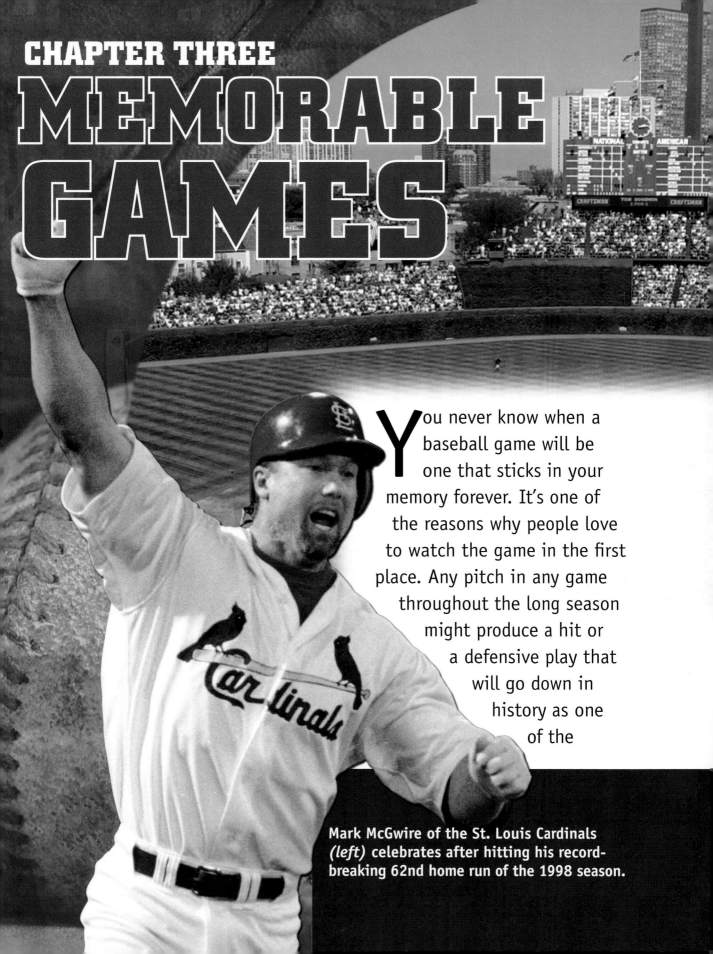

CHAPTER THREE
MEMORABLE GAMES

You never know when a baseball game will be one that sticks in your memory forever. It's one of the reasons why people love to watch the game in the first place. Any pitch in any game throughout the long season might produce a hit or a defensive play that will go down in history as one of the

Mark McGwire of the St. Louis Cardinals *(left)* celebrates after hitting his record-breaking 62nd home run of the 1998 season.

greatest ever. This chapter takes a look at some memorable moments from recent games involving teams in the NL Central division.

Big Mac and the Single-Season Home Run Record

The 1998 season was one of the most exciting in baseball history, thanks to two sluggers in the National League Central division. As the summer headed toward fall, Mark McGwire of the St. Louis Cardinals and Sammy Sosa of the Chicago Cubs were on pace to break one of the most coveted records in sports: baseball's single-season home run record. Roger Maris had held the record—61 homers—since 1961, a span of 37 years.

McGwire edged ahead of Sosa as the season entered its final weeks. Then, as luck would have it, Sosa and the Cubs were scheduled to visit St. Louis on September 7–8 to play two games against the Cardinals. In the first game, McGwire hit home run number 61 to tie Maris. In the next day's game, in McGwire's second time at bat, he cranked the historic blast, a laser-like line drive that barely cleared the left-field fence. As the capacity crowd went wild, McGwire himself was so excited that he missed first base and had to go back and step on the bag before completing his record-setting trip around the bases! McGwire would go on to hit eight more home runs that year, for a total of 70. Sosa finished with 66.

The Mother's Day Gift

In honor of Mother's Day in 2006, players from around the major leagues used pink bats as part of a campaign to raise awareness for breast cancer. Many players used the special bats on their first trip to the plate only to switch to their regular bats later in the game. However, the Milwaukee Brewers' Bill Hall stayed with his pink bat throughout the game. In his first three trips to the plate, the bat didn't seem to have any special magic in it—Hall struck out three times. But the Brewers' infielder didn't want to disappoint his mother, Vergie Hall, who had traveled 10 hours by car from her home in Mississippi just to see her son play in Milwaukee that day. Fortunately for Hall, he would get a chance to redeem himself using the special bat bearing his mother's name.

Bill Hall of the Milwaukee Brewers launches his game-winning home run on Mother's Day, May 14, 2006.

Hall came to the plate in the 10th inning, with the game tied 5–5. In an ending that could have been dreamed up by a Hollywood scriptwriter, Hall hit a walk-off home run over the left-field wall, giving the Brewers a 6–5 win. The bat was later auctioned off for more than $25,000, with the proceeds going to breast cancer research. The high bidder was actually Brewers team owner Mark Attanasio, who in turn gave the bat to Vergie Hall as a gift.

The Dad Slam

Friday May 28, 2004, will almost certainly remain the most memorable day of Rob Mackowiak's life. At 11 o'clock in the morning, Mackowiak's wife, Jennifer, gave birth to the couple's first son. After spending the morning in the hospital, Mackowiak headed to the ballpark to play in a doubleheader for the Pittsburgh Pirates. He arrived just one hour before the first game was to begin.

Mackowiak struggled in the first game. He was 0 for 4 in his first four appearances at the plate. But then, with the game tied 5–5 in the bottom of the ninth inning, Mackowiak provided his son with the perfect birthday present. With the bases loaded and two outs, he stepped to the plate and connected for a walk-off grand slam, giving the Pirates a 9–5 win. As teammates swarmed the new father at home plate, it seemed like the perfect day. But Mackowiak's big day wasn't over yet.

After hitting a game-winning home run, Rob Mackowiak *(right)* is greeted at home plate by excited Pittsburgh Pirates teammates.

In the second game of the doubleheader, Mackowiak again stepped up to the plate in a crucial situation. It was the ninth inning, and his Pirates were down by two runs. Incredibly, with a runner on first base, Mackowiak smashed another home run, tying the game at 4. The Pirates eventually won in extra innings. Mackowiak's impressive stats for the day were two home runs, six RBI, two Pirates victories, and one newborn son.

Kerry Wood Strikes Out 20 Batters

It takes a lot of guts to be a Cubs fan. First of all, it has been 100 years since the team won the World Series. Second, going to a game at famous Wrigley Field can sometimes be a real test of endurance, as cold winds whip off Lake Michigan, just a few blocks east of the park. On a cold, rainy day in early May 1998, less than 16,000 hearty fans made it to Wrigley for an afternoon game. Fortunately for them, their bravery and perseverance was rewarded with a game for the history books.

On the pitcher's mound that day was the Cubs much-hyped 20-year-old rookie, Kerry Wood. He was starting in just his fifth major league game. Wood's day wouldn't be easy, for he was facing the defending Central division champions, the Houston Astros. Their batting order was one of the most potent in the National League, featuring the Killer B's: Craig Biggio, Derek Bell, and Jeff Bagwell. In the first inning, surprisingly, Wood made the Killer B's look like cream puffs, fanning all three of them. And the strikeouts kept coming.

By the time the ninth inning rolled around, Wood had struck out 18 batters. The major league record of 20 strikeouts in a nine-inning

game was within his reach. With the small crowd on its feet, he struck out two more Astros in the ninth to tie the record. In more than 100 years of professional baseball, the feat has been accomplished by only three pitchers: Roger Clemens (twice), Randy Johnson, and Kerry Wood.

D'oh, Bartman!

In 2003, the Cubs were five outs away from making it to their first World Series in almost 50 years. Leading by a score of 3–0 in game 6 of the NLCS, Cubs pitcher Mark Prior got Marlins batter Luis Castillo to lift a harmless foul ball near the left-field line. As Cubs left fielder Moises Alou moved in to make a play, a spectator named Steve Bartman reached out and deflected the ball with his hand, preventing Alou from making the catch. Castillo eventually drew a walk, and before the inning was over, the Marlins had scored eight runs. Florida won game 6 and went on to win game 7 the following night.

For Bartman, a lifelong and loyal Cubs fan, life became a nightmare. A half-century of fan frustration poured out on him like venom. He had to be escorted from the stadium by security guards and then had to go into seclusion for months.

In 2004, the ball that Bartman touched was blown up with explosives in a special ceremony in Chicago. Some felt that this symbolic event helped to erase the feeling that the Cubs are cursed. Nevertheless, the name Bartman is one that will live in infamy on the North Side of Chicago.

Unfortunate Cubs fan Steve Bartman *(in black shirt)* interferes with a foul pop-up in game 6 of the 2003 National League Championship Series.

Six Astros Pitchers, One No-Hitter

No ballpark has seen more historic moments than famed Yankee Stadium in New York. On June 11, 2003, the Houston Astros were in the Big Apple for an interleague game. When it was over, their pitching staff accomplished something that had never been done at Yankee Stadium— or any other stadium in the history of baseball, for that matter.

The night did not start out well for the Astros. After retiring the first three Yankees in the first inning, their starting pitcher Roy Oswalt left the game with an injury. In stepped Pete Munro, who kept the Yankees hitless over the next two and two-thirds innings. Kirk Sarloos followed Munro and retired all four batters he faced. Brad Lidge came into the game in the sixth inning and proceeded to pitch two innings without allowing a hit. Next up was Octavio Dotel, who struck out the side in the eighth inning.

In the last inning, Houston brought in their closer Billy Wagner, who recorded the final three outs in order, sealing the Astros' 8–0 victory. For the first time in Major League Baseball history, six different pitchers combined to throw a no-hitter.

CHAPTER FOUR

BALLPARKS AND TRADITIONS

With a long history, time-honored traditions, and die-hard fans, the NL Central is one of the best divisions in the major leagues. The teams all play in the central part of the United States, but each club, with its fans, ballparks, and traditions, is unique to its city.

Chicago Cubs

The Cubs franchise was one of the original eight teams of the National

Junction Jack *(left)* is the Texas-sized jackrabbit mascot of the Houston Astros.

League. Early Cubs teams enjoyed great success, winning back-to-back World Series titles in 1907 and 1908. Unfortunately for Cubs fans, as of 2007, the 1908 title was the most recent one! In 1916, the Cubs played their first game at Weeghman Park, which was renamed Wrigley Field in 1926.

Wrigley Field

Location: Chicago, Illinois
Opened for baseball in: 1916 (first Cubs game)
Surface: Natural grass
Seating capacity: 41,160

Wrigley Field is the second-oldest major league ballpark still in operation, after Boston's Fenway Park (1912). Its age makes it one of the most intimate and friendly parks in base-ball. Wrigley is well known for its unique brick outfield walls, which have been covered in their famous ivy since 1937.

People on the North Side of Chicago, where Wrigley is located, love baseball and their Cubs.

At Chicago's Wrigley Field, spectator seating is not limited to the bleachers inside the ballpark. These fans *(above, top)* are enjoying the game from nearby rooftops.

However, with such a long record of World Series futility, many fans focus instead on the fun experience of going to the game. For this reason, a visit to Wrigley Field can feel more like attending a party than a ball game. Often, a particularly good time is had by fans seated atop buildings on Waveland Avenue, beyond the left-field bleachers.

For those who really care whether the Cubs win or lose, a unique tradition at Wrigley Field is the flying of a special flag atop the scoreboard after a game. A white flag with a blue W lets everyone know that the Cubs won; a blue flag with a white L indicates a loss.

For decades, Wrigley Field hosted only day games. However, in 1988, lighting was finally installed for night games.

Wrigley was once the home of one of baseball's most beloved announcers, Harry Carey. Throughout the 1980s and 1990s, Cubs fans always looked forward to the seventh-inning stretch. That was when Carey would grab a microphone and lead them in a rousing—and often out-of-tune—rendition of "Take Me Out to the Ball Game."

Cincinnati Reds

The Reds won World Series titles in 1919 and 1940. The team spent many years without another world title until the mid-1970s. At that time, Cincinnati fielded an impressive team known as the Big Red Machine. This crew, led by Pete Rose, Joe Morgan, Johnny Bench, and Tony Perez, won back-to-back World Series titles in 1975 and 1976. The franchise won its most recent World Series in 1990.

From 1970 to 1999, the Reds played at Riverfront Stadium (renamed Cinergy Field in 1996), a building they shared with the Cincinnati Bengals of the National Football League. Cinergy Field was leveled in 2002 to make room for a brand-new park.

Great American Ball Park

Location: Cincinnati, Ohio
Opened in: 2003
Surface: Natural grass
Seating capacity: 42,941

Great American Ball Park is located on the banks of the Ohio River.
Designed for baseball only, the park opened to much praise in 2003.

The Ohio River is visible beyond the bleachers of Great American Ball Park in
Cincinnati. The state of Kentucky lies on the opposite bank.

It features a massive scoreboard in left field, which keeps fans up to date on the game they are watching, as well as all other games in the major leagues. In keeping with the park's riverboat theme, two giant smokestacks in center field launch fireworks and spew steam when Reds players hit home runs. For many years, the Reds mascot was Mr. Red, a character with a huge baseball head. Since the move to Great American Ball Park, duties have been fulfilled by the team's new mascots, Mr. Redlegs and Gapper.

Houston Astros

The original Houston ball club was called the Colt .45s. They entered the National League in 1962. About that time, Houston was the bustling headquarters of NASA and the U.S. space program. To take advantage of the city's high-tech reputation, team owners changed the name of the team to "Astros" in 1965. That year, they also began playing in the Astrodome, a futuristic-looking domed stadium.

The Astros didn't win much in their first few decades of existence, but Houston fans remained loyal, rooting for stars including Nolan Ryan, César Cedeño, Joe Niekro, and Mike Scott. Astros fans could be spotted miles away, with their brightly colored, striped uniforms. In 2000, the Astros moved from the aging Astrodome to their new stadium, today named Minute Maid Park.

Minute Maid Park
Location: Houston, Texas
Opened in: 2000
Surface: Natural grass
Seating capacity: 40,950

Houstonians playfully call Minute Maid Park "the Juice Box." The state-of-the-art ballpark has a retractable roof. When the hot, humid Texas weather gets unbearable, the roof can be closed and the air conditioning turned on to make conditions much more comfortable for fans and players alike. Minute Maid Park is loaded with fun, unique features. First, there is a very short, hitter-friendly left-field fence, which makes for high-scoring games. There's also Tal's Hill, an inclined patch of grass in straightaway center field that has a flagpole at the top.

Several unique features of Houston's Minute Maid Park are visible in this view: the steam locomotive, above the wall in left-center field; Tal's Hill, beyond the warning track in center field; and the retracted roof, above the scoreboard in right field.

Another great feature of the park is Union Station, originally built in 1911. Today, the renovated station is the main entrance to the park. Trains don't pull into Union Station anymore, but Houston's history as a great Western railway city is recalled by the park's full-size replica of a nineteenth-century steam locomotive. Whenever a Houston player hits a home run, the train blows its whistle and runs along an 800-foot track above the left-field fence. Fans looking to satisfy their hunger can nosh on local specialties, including sausages, BBQ, and Tex-Mex food.

Milwaukee Brewers

The Milwaukee Brewers enjoyed their best season in 1982, when they were aligned with the American League East division. That year, the team went all the way to the World Series, losing to the St. Louis Cardinals in seven intense games. Both teams now play in the NL Central, and you can believe that Brewers fans are looking for their team to avenge that loss. In 2001, the Brewers left their outdated County Stadium for their new digs in Miller Park.

Miller Park
Location: Milwaukee, Wisconsin
Opened in: 2001
Surface: Natural grass
Seating capacity: 41,900

Springtime in Milwaukee can be chilly, so the Brewers' new park was designed with a unique, fan-shaped convertible roof for better climate control. Like St. Louis and Chicago, Milwaukee has a proud tradition of brewing beer. (After all, the "Miller" in "Miller Park" is for the Miller

Brewing Company.) When the Brewers played at County Stadium, their home-run celebration became very popular. Every time a Brewer homered, mascot Bernie Brewer came out of his chalet and slid down into a huge beer mug to release balloons stored inside. However, when the Brewers moved in to Miller Park, Bernie became a more kid-friendly character and lost his sudsy theme. Now, he comes out of his dugout and slides down a bobsled-like chute to a platform at the bottom. To mark a Brewers win, fireworks explode above the center-field fence.

The Great Sausage Race

Wisconsin has been a favorite destination of German and Polish immigrants since the 1800s. Early arrivals to the area brought with them their love of traditional beer brewing and also their appreciation of German-style sausages. This part of the region's heritage can be seen at Brewers home games in the Great Sausage Race. For this crowd-pleasing event, park employees wearing huge foam sausage costumes come onto the field between innings. The race now features five meaty contestants: Bratwurst (#1), Polish Sausage (#2), Italian Sausage (#3), Hot Dog (#4), and a recent Spanish-flavor addition, Chorizo (#5). The sausages race around the dirt track of the infield, starting near third base and finishing near the first-base dugout. Fans have a great time rooting for their favorite character, erupting in cheers and laughter when the winning sausage crosses the finish line.

The five costumed contestants line up for the ever-popular Great Sausage Race at Miller Park in Milwaukee.

St. Louis Cardinals

St. Louis is the National League's most successful franchise. In their long history, the Cardinals have won 17 National League pennants. Their 10 World Series titles (the most recent won in 2006) are second only to the 27 titles won by the New York Yankees.

From 1966 to 2006, the Cardinals played at "old" Busch Stadium, in downtown St. Louis. Today, the team plays in "new" Busch Stadium, a different structure with the same name. From 1970 to 1995, old Busch Stadium had artificial turf, which determined the players the Cardinals acquired and the type of ball they played. From 1980 to 1990, for instance, the Cards built winning teams based on a combination of speed, pitching, and a great defense anchored by their perennial All-Star shortstop, Ozzie Smith.

St. Louis loves its "Redbirds." In fact, since 2006, about 3.5 million fans have flocked to new Busch Stadium each year to see the Cardinals play. For every home game, the stadium is a sea of Cardinal red.

Busch Stadium

Location: St. Louis, Missouri
Opened in: 2006
Surface: Natural grass
Seating capacity: 49,676

The new park was built over much of the same area where the old stadium stood. Unlike old Busch Stadium, the new one has a break in the center-field bleachers that allows fans to view the St. Louis skyline, including the city's most recognizable structure, the Gateway Arch.
(For a panorama view of the park, see pages 4–5.)

GLOSSARY

analytical Skilled in using thinking or reasoning.

clamor To shout noisily.

contend To struggle for.

cornerstone Foundation or basic element.

frenzied Marked by intense, wild activity.

hype To promote, usually with unrealistic claims of excellence.

milestone Significant point in development.

nimble Quick and light in motion; agile.

pedigree Distinguished ancestry or lineage.

plateau Level of achievement.

RBI In baseball, shorthand for run batted in.

redeem To atone for or make good.

seclusion An isolated place.

slew Army or large number.

spew To emit or send forth.

unique One-of-a-kind; distinctive.

wild card team In baseball, the second-place team, from any division, with the best record.

zealous Passionate; enthusiastic.

FOR MORE INFORMATION

Major League Baseball
The Office of the Commissioner of Baseball
245 Park Avenue, 31st Floor
New York, NY 10167
(212) 931-7800
Web site: http://www.mlb.com
The commissioner's office oversees all aspects of Major League
    Baseball.

National Baseball Hall of Fame and Museum
25 Main Street
Cooperstown, NY 13326
(888) HALL-OF-FAME (425-5633)
Web site: http://www.baseballhalloffame.org
The National Baseball Hall of Fame and Museum celebrates
    and preserves the history of baseball.

Negro Leagues Baseball Museum
1616 East 18th Street
Kansas City, MO 64108
(816) 221-1920
Web site: http://www.nlbm.com
The Negro Leagues Baseball Museum honors great African
    American baseball players who were once excluded from
    Major League Baseball.

(Note: Links to official individual team Web sites are available at the Rosenlinks URL, listed below)

Web Sites

Due to the changing nature of Internet links, Rosen Publishing has developed an online list of Web sites related to the subject of this book. This site is updated regularly. Please use this link to access the list:

http://www.rosenlinks.com/imlb/nalc

FOR FURTHER READING

Altergott, Hannah. *Great Teams in Baseball History*. Milwaukee, WI: Raintree Publishing, 2006.

Christopher, Matt. *World Series: Legendary Sports Events*. New York, NY: Little, Brown & Company, 2007.

Gilbert, Sara. *The Story of the Milwaukee Brewers*. Mankato, MN: Creative Education, 2007.

Golenbock, Peter. *The Spirit of St. Louis: A History of the St. Louis Cardinals and Browns*. New York, NY: Peter Morrow, 2000.

Lipsyte, Robert. *Heroes of Baseball: The Men Who Made It America's Favorite Game*. New York, NY: Atheneum Books for Young Readers, 2006.

McCollister, John. *Bucs: The Story of the Pittsburgh Pirates*. Lenexa, KS: Addax Publishers, 2002.

Stewart, Mark. *Chicago Cubs* (Team Spirit Book). Chicago, IL: Norwood House, 2008.

Stewart, Mark. *Cincinnati Reds* (Team Spirit Book). Chicago, IL: Norwood House, 2008.

Thorn, John, Phil Birnbaum, Bill Deane, et al., eds. *Total Baseball, Completely Revised and Updated: The Ultimate Baseball Encyclopedia*. Wilmington, DE: SportClassic Books, 2004.

Vecsey, George. *Baseball: A History of America's Favorite Game*. New York, NY: Random House Publishing Group, 2006.

BIBLIOGRAPHY

Associated Press. "Dad Slam: Pirate Hits GW HR After Son's Birth." 2008. Retrieved May 20, 2008 (http://nbcsports. msnbc.com/id/5088118/#storyContinued).

Baseball-Reference.com. Multiple pages. Retrieved May 11–21, 2008 (http://www.baseball-reference.com).

Black Book Partners. Multiple pages. Retrieved June 2–6, 2008 (http://jockbio.com).

de Jesus Ortiz, José. "6 Astros Pitchers Combine to Handcuff Yankees." *Houston Chronicle*, June 12, 2003. Retrieved June 13, 2008 (http://www.astrosdaily.com/history/ 20030611).

Gammons, Peter, Gary Gillette, and Pete Palmer. *The ESPN Encyclopedia. 5th ed.* (ESPN Baseball Encyclopedia). New York, NY: Sterling Publishing Co., 2008.

Koppett, Leonard. *Koppett's Concise History of Major League Baseball*. New York, NY: Carroll & Graf Publishers, 2004.

Major League Baseball. "Attanasio Goes to Bat for Mother's Day." Retrieved May 20, 2008 (http://mlb.mlb.com/ news/press_releases/press_release.jsp?ymd= 20060707&content_id=1544650&vkey=pr_mil& fext=.jsp&c_id=mil).

Major League Baseball. "Busch Stadium: Home of the Cardinals." Retrieved May 20, 2008 (http://cardinals.mlb.com/stl/ ballpark).

Major League Baseball. "No More Steaks for Fielder." Retrieved July 9, 2008 (http://mlb.mlb.com/news/article.jsp?ymd=20080221& content_id=2383789&vkey=spt2008news&fext=.jsp&c_id=mil).

Major League Baseball. "Racing Sausages." Retrieved May 21, 2008 (http://milwaukee.brewers.mlb.com/mil/fan_forum/racing_ sausages.jsp).

Major League Baseball. "Wood's Smoke." Retrieved May 20, 2008 (http://mlb.mlb.com/mlb/baseballs_best/mlb_bb_gamepage. jsp?story_page=bb_98reg_050698_houchc).

Munsey and Suppes. Multiple pages. Ballparks.com, 1996–2008. Retrieved May 11–21 (http://www.ballparks.com/baseball/ index.htm).

Pahigian, Joshua, and Kevin O'Connell. *The Ultimate Baseball Road-Trip: A Fan's Guide to Major League Baseball*. Guilford, CT: Lyons Press, 2004.

Rolaids Relief Man Award Site. "Past Winners." McNeil-PPC, Inc., 2007. Retrieved April 1, 2008 (http://www.rolaidsreliefman.com/ pastwinners.aspx).

INDEX

About the Author

Ed Eck is a writer and television producer for the world's biggest cable sports network. For his work, he has interviewed dozens of baseball players, managers, and team executives. Eck has also covered hundreds of Major League Baseball games, including the National League and American League championships series and the World Series. He grew up outside of New York City and currently resides with his family in Connecticut.

Photo Credits

Cover, pp. 1, 7, 14, 25, 32 (background) Jonathan Daniel/Getty Images; cover (center) Stephen Dunn/Getty Images; cover (insets top to bottom), p. 1 (insets) Jamie Squire/Getty Images, Jonathan Daniel/Getty Images, Rick Stewart/Getty Images, Doug Benc/Getty Images, Dilip Vishwanat/Getty Images, Marc Serota/Getty Images; pp. 4–5 Dilip Vishwanat/Getty Images; pp. 5, 12, 14, 18, 20, 24, 33, 35, 39 Jonathan Daniel/Getty Images; p. 7 Focus on Sport/Getty Images; pp. 9, 27, 28, 30 © AP Images; p. 17 Eliot J. Schechter/ Getty Images; p. 25 Peter Newcomb/AFP/Getty Images; p. 32 MLB Photos via Getty Images; p. 37 Bill Baptist/Getty Images.

Designer: Sam Zavieh; Editor: Christopher Roberts
Photo Researcher: Cindy Reiman